HEALING TREES

HEALING TREES

A POCKET GUIDE TO FOREST BATHING

BEN PAGE

MANDALA

San Rafael • Los Angeles • London

See the world as yourself.
Have faith in the way things are.
Love the world as yourself;
Then you can care for all things.

—Lao-tzu

Dedicated to Ric.

CONTENTS

A NOTE FOR THE READER

In exploring Forest Bathing, we are asking ourselves a simple question: How do we create authentic relationships with nature? This book cannot answer that question because all relationships are unique; it can, however, help you to find your own answers through your own practice. You might also consider attending a facilitated Forest Bathing walk; you may notice that you experience the practice differently in the company of a guide.

This book wants to be read outside, so that you are not only experiencing the ideas expressed on the page but are also experiencing the sensations of nature at the same time. It also wants to be read slowly, so that you will practice patience and remember how not to rush things that move at their own pace. Let the experience of reading this book reflect the ethos of this practice; move through it slowly, with your senses awakened and with an open heart.

Before you read the first chapter, you are invited to find a *sit spot*. A sit spot is somewhere in nature where your body wants to sit, a place you will spend time with through many seasons. It could be in your backyard, or a local park, or really anywhere you like. It helps for it to be somewhere convenient, so that you don't have to spend a lot of time commuting there; choose a place that is comfortable and easily accessible.

If you allow it, your sit spot will become a good mentor in the practice of Forest Bathing. Just sitting there, simply relaxing into the moment, will help you understand things that this book can only attempt to describe. It's good to spend at least thirty minutes there, but sometimes you may want to sit for longer. At the end of each chapter, there is a prompt for you to take to your sit spot. You might wait to read it until after you have arrived at your sit spot, so that you will receive it spontaneously.

Before you consider the prompt, take some time to settle into your body. Notice any sensations you are experiencing, then begin observing the world around you. What does it look like, feel like, sound like, smell like? You may choose to explore the prompt in your journal, or maybe just in your imagination. Don't think about it too much;

let the question move organically through your mind and body, and then simply listen to your heart.

Whatever arises is yours to do with what you will; there are no right or wrong answers. And when you run out of prompts, perhaps you will return to your sit spot and receive new prompts informed by your relationship to the nature of that space. This is how a sit spot can become an infinite adventure and a lifelong relationship. The more time you spend there, the deeper your relationship will grow; this has nothing to do with outcomes, and everything to do with good process. Trust that your body will guide you; you only need to give it time.

As you read this book, allow it to be more like a series of stories than a dogmatic truth. You don't have to agree or disagree with these stories; you can just let them be what they are. All learning and growth emerges from the tension between our existing stories and new ideas, but you are not obligated to learn anything or grow in any way that does not serve you. You can hold these stories in your hands, but your hands must first be empty; try to set aside what you may think of as rigid truths and invite yourself to be curious about what more may exist.

If you are willing to hold stories in your hands and examine them with curiosity, then perhaps you will grasp them. But grasp not too tightly, as these stories are more like water than stones; they are not meant to be static for too long. Let them move and watch where they go; whatever returns is the lesson meant for your attention.

Ultimately, I hope that this book inspires you to co-author your own stories with the land that you live on, the places you visit, your own body, and all of nature. Because they are authentically yours, it is these stories that should become your guide to Forest Bathing. This book is about Forest Bathing, but it is not a substitute for Forest Bathing; only you can discover your practice.

A NOTE FOR THE READER

FOREWORD

Good poetry has the uncanny capacity to put into words that which cannot be said. Its meaning arises not in the words themselves, but in a felt sense evoked by the power of the poem. Ben Page shows us how we can work with the forest to create a kind of poetry that reveals its meaning through the unique ways in which the natural world ignites our imaginations. In this book, he offers ten invitations that we can take into the woods when we are ready to hear the forest speaking in its language beyond words.

Experienced thus, the voice of the forest has healing qualities. It soothes the soul and quiets the busy mind. There are many approaches to forest therapy, but the one that Page offers has the virtue of simplicity. It is well within the reach of anyone who is capable of the act of simply sitting. No goals, no distractions, just you and what surrounds you. Perhaps those who have this capacity are not as many as there once were. But it's not so hard to do, and this book is a reliable guide for those who wish to explore the experience.

This is a practice that attunes you to the inner rhythms of your mind as well as the outer rhythms of the land, its diurnal and seasonal changes. Things don't happen quickly; the ways in which you are affected by a Forest Bathing experience may not become apparent to you for hours, days, or weeks afterward. There is often a subtlety to the benefits. I cannot speak for what you will experience, nor does Ben, but I can tell what this practice has meant for me. It has been a journey of slowly coming home to myself.

A few days ago, I was undertaking a journey, a daylong drive. I had driven a hundred miles or so when I realized that I was travelling more lightly than I had been recently. What I had left behind were things that I did not need. Stripped down to the essentials, I was free to be closer to the essence of myself. Pondering this realization, I connected it to a Forest Bathing walk I had taken two days before. Wandering down a hillside on the faint trails left by animals, I was in a sorrowful mood when I came to a small ravine where I felt invited to sit. My body felt at ease. Across the ravine was an old bay tree with some of its tangled roots exposed by the erosion of the ravine's wall. In the patterns on the bark and the way the roots were arranged, I saw a face with a goofy, lighthearted smile. Was this an image from the imaginal world, a revelation of a listening presence? I decided it was, and so I spoke to the tree, telling it of recent events in my life, of changes ahead of me, of questions I had. At a remove from any human presence, I felt free to speak with total honesty, to be transparent so that the tree might gaze into my heart. The gaze of the tree is no different than the gaze of our own inner knowing, and two days later I realized that by confiding in nature I had lightened my emotional load, just as earlier I had lightened the load of things I carried with me.

This is a book that understands how the power of the forest animates our imaginations and brings us home to ourselves. My advice for how to use this book is simple: slowly, one chapter at a time, and in the company of the forest. Take the sit spot prompts with you.

They are well crafted and will be reliable friends. May your journey through this book and on the trails be beautiful.

Amos Clifford
Founder, Association of Nature and
Forest Therapy Guides and Programs
Author, *Your Guide to Forest Bathing*

INTRODUCTION

HOW DID I COME TO KNOW FOREST BATHING?

When I am asked about where my journey began, I cannot help but think back to the beginning of this lifetime. In those days, there were fewer distractions. I remember navigating forests by moonlight and building fires, swimming in creeks and climbing mountains. I remember being on my hands and knees in the dirt, spotting crocuses coming up in the spring and the scent of fallen leaves in the autumn. I remember what fresh snow tasted like and the sound of the peeping frogs at night and the texture of the lamb's ears that grew behind our neighbor's house. I remember the power and simplicity of those experiences. As a child, it was reflexive; I didn't need to be taught how to experience what is now called "Forest Bathing." Back then, I just knew it as play.

And then I got older and life got faster, more demanding, more stressful. I acquired new interests, had more homework, more extracurriculars, more, more, more of everything, and always less time. I felt there was a lot of pressure to go to a "good college," so that I could get a "good job," so that I could have a "good life," and so everything became oriented around becoming the best version of myself. Life was about striving, and there was no time to watch the trees or listen to the wind anymore.

I remember that was a stressful time. A big part of the stress was that all of a sudden, I held the idea that I had to be special, that to be meaningful in life was the height of achievement. I remember feeling like the concept of my potential was always out of reach, and I didn't understand who I was. So I kept building up this idea of myself that I had been told would be meaningful, hoping that someday it would make me whole.

In that time, I still appreciated nature, but my relationship to it had changed. I still thought it was beautiful, but it was a beauty I observed from a distance, in the way one might appreciate a painting in a gallery. I lost touch with the intimate connections to place that I had known as a child and the way that the beings of the earth could be more than beautiful objects, but a vast community of friends.

Yet the world works in mysterious ways, and I did return to that perception eventually. When I was a senior in high school, I had an incredible teacher named Bill Schechter. I took a class with Bill in which we read Thoreau's *Walden* and we read the last chapter at sunrise, before school, at the site of Thoreau's cabin. This was a place not far from where I lived and was somewhere I had walked many times.

I remember us in the golden light of early morning, reading the final lines. And then Bill turned to us and said something like, "Well, I have to go to work now. If I don't show up, they'll fire me. But you're all seniors in high school, and if I were you, I'd cut class and take a walk around this pond. What Thoreau was writing about was his experience of this place. But you'll never have Thoreau's experience of these woods; you can only read about it. You can, however, find a way to have your own experience. Don't let Thoreau be the expert of this place! You will find your own relationship here." And that's exactly what we all did. We went on our own journeys to find our own knowing, our own experience of the place called Walden.

I remember it was like waking up from a trance. Wandering slowly through that forest, having permission from Bill to rebel against time scarcity and to abandon the idea of Thoreau's expertise, I started to repair my

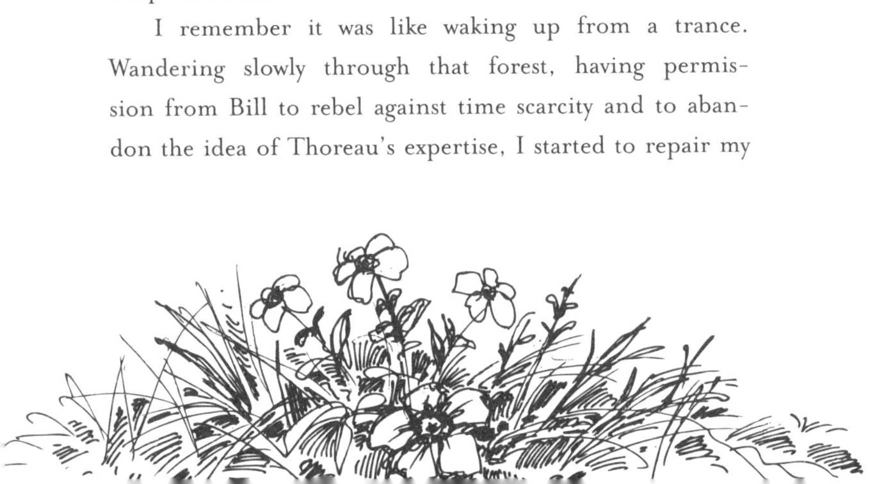

relationship to that place and the beings who lived there. I sat with trees who I had spent time with as a child but had not visited in ages. I heard the sounds of the morning that I never heard because I was always in school at that time. I remember a squirrel watching me for a while, and realizing that the forest could see me here, that the earth was gazing back. It wasn't like a beautiful painting or a line from a famous book; it was a lived experience of presence and relationship.

I remember on that walk, noticing how vivid and detailed everything was. I recall asking myself, "How much of this world have I been missing? How distracted have I been that I have not seen what is right in front of me this whole time?" And it wasn't just that I was sensing differently, I was feeling differently too. I felt like I was seeing the inner beauty of nature, not just appreciating the beauty on the surface.

In that moment, I felt alive. I stopped searching for who I was and became intimate with the reality of what I was. It wasn't abstract, or meaningful in a way I could describe; it was personal and direct and ephemeral in its beauty. That was the first time I remember holding the conscious awareness of what I had been doing all throughout my childhood. I was building a real relationship to place, with nothing more than the intelligence of my own body and the permission to give myself time to explore without any agenda or expectations. I like to think that was my first conscious experience of Forest Bathing.

Many years later, I was trained in the second cohort of forest therapy guides by the Association of Nature and Forest Therapy, and I then became a trainer. I spent five years travelling around the world, training guides all across the United States and Canada and as far away as Norway, Costa Rica, New Zealand, Australia, and England. I was and still am incredibly humbled by how teaching something requires you to be a student of it as well, and I was mentored in reciprocity from every guide I worked with and every place I spent time with.

No matter where I went, when I was in nature, I felt that I was loved unconditionally because I was nature. And I learned to love nature in that way as well because I started seeing that everything in nature was beautiful and worthy of love. And that feeling, that relationship with the world, became my deepest aspiration as I travelled; I wanted to fall in love over and over again with every landscape on earth. And then, the coronavirus came and everything stopped.

Interestingly, this is where my practice really deepened. I had to figure out how to practice without going anywhere. This is when I began to truly understand that I carry the forest within me, that my body is nature. As long as I could learn to be right here, right now, connected to my body and connected to my senses, I could be Forest Bathing anywhere, anytime. When the whole world slowed down to a near standstill, I finally came back to the most intimate nature of my life: my own body and the land I live upon.

This is why I'm writing this book. Through Forest Bathing, I hope that you will remember that you are nature, and that being nature is quite extraordinary in ways that require absolutely no specialness. When we let go of our specialness, we begin to understand that we don't have to prove ourselves worthy of existence. We don't need to be special because we are part of something incredible: this world, this moment in time and space. Through this sense of belonging, we remember what love really means. We are called to know, not intellectually but deep in our hearts, what it is like to be unconditionally accepted so that we can reciprocate that love toward the world in return. We are like mountains, or wind, or waves, or flowers; we're just here, never alone, connected to everything and we are enough. We are not here to sit in judgment, but to be humbled by the force of love that binds this world together.

Sit Spot
PROMPT 1

As you sit, invite patience to sit with you.
Notice what unfolds around and within you.

CHAPTER 1

WHAT IS FOREST BATHING?

Dr. Qing Li, one of the world's foremost experts in forest medicine, describes *shinrin-yoku* in his book, *Forest Bathing: How Trees Can Help You Find Health and Happiness*: "How to do shinrin-yoku in the park: Leave behind your phone, camera, music, and any other distractions. Leave behind your expectations. Slow down; forget about the time. Come into the present moment. Find a spot to sit—on the grass, beside a tree, or on a park bench. Notice what you can hear and see. Notice what you feel. Stay for two hours if possible." It seems so simple, yet beneath the simplicity, there is an ocean of nuance.

Forest Bathing arose in Japan in the 1980s as the country was going through a massive cultural shift. The combined effects of rapid urbanization and the emergence of the information technology economy introduced the Japanese workforce to unprecedented levels of pollution, stress, and mounting digital addiction. To compound this, the work culture of the new economy was extremely taxing—physically, mentally, and emotionally. After noticing that workers were getting sick and dying of stress-induced exhaustion, the Japanese even coined a word for such a phenomenon: *karoshi* (過労死), meaning "death by overwork."

The emergence of this high tech, high stress, urban lifestyle was closely correlated to an enormous spike in cancer and autoimmune disease. In response to this public health crisis, the Japanese government began several research projects to explore possible solutions. Shinrin-yoku, a nature immersion practice pioneered by the Japanese Ministry of Agriculture, Forestry and Fisheries, was one of these projects. The term was coined in 1982 to describe a method for curbing the dangerous health impacts of urban living and revitalizing the economies of rural prefectures in the countryside. Today, millions of Japanese citizens walk on designated shinrin-yoku trails every year for their health and well-being.

Dr. Li explains that the term "Forest Bathing" comes from the translation of the Japanese *shinrin-yoku* (森林浴). Shinrin translates to *forest* and yoku to *bath*, hence *Forest Bathing*. What the Japanese are referring to is a sort of double entendre and a play on the word *bathing*; therefore, shinrin-yoku has two parallel meanings that derive from the same translation.

The first meaning is "bathing in the forest atmosphere." In this first sense, the *bathing* refers to a literal immersion into the atmosphere of the forest. Dr. Li describes it as a sort of *natural aromatherapy*. When we take a walk in the forest, the air is rich in organic compounds released from trees and other plant life. As we walk through the forest, bathing in this compound-rich air, we absorb these substances by simply inhaling them, which benefits us by healing our bodies and boosting our immune systems.

The second meaning is "taking in the forest through our senses." In this second meaning, the *bathing* refers to the sensory experience of simply being in the forest in a slow and relaxed manner. In this way, it's a lot like a similar activity people engage in called *sunbathing*. When people go sunbathing, they are simply experiencing the physical relationship between sunlight and their bodies. If you picture what it looks like when someone is sunbathing, there's nothing complicated or intellectual about it; they're simply relaxing in the warmth of sunlight. So, when people go Forest Bathing, they are simply relaxing and experiencing the physical sensations of being in the forest. It might help to think of it as the difference between taking a quick shower and a long, luxurious bath. It's not about efficiency; it is about intentionally luxuriating in restfulness.

When considering the origins of shinrin-yoku, it is important not to overlook the fact that Indigenous Japanese culture, informed by Shinto and Zen Buddhism, had a long history of nature immersion practices before the 1980s, and that the Japanese were arguably doing something similar to what is now called Forest Bathing for centuries. We can sense these ancient influences in Dr. Li's instructions to "leave behind your expectations"; "come into the present moment"; and "notice what you feel." Such sentiments can also help us understand Forest Bathing as a contemplative practice that extends the metaphor of bathing to include a third meaning: the act of bathing in this *present moment.*

While Forest Bathing, instead of trying to freeze or capture a moment by describing it with thoughts, we experience reality fluidly, as if we are bathing in a river of time, letting each moment rush by and through our bodies without attachment or analysis. We don't try to hold on to the moments and sensations as they arise and fade; we simply relax into a state of fluid attention, noticing whatever comes up, undistracted by what has passed and what will come next. When we experience this bathing in presence, we return to the original mind, which is the intelligence of the entire body, the intelligence of our inner nature. In my own Forest Bathing, I find that this third definition is as important as the two more commonly known translations, and that all three together provide a wonderfully nuanced approach to the way we actually practice.

Forest Bathing invites us to experience the world immediately and intimately, and it is in this way that we begin to cultivate real relationships. Real relationships are not characterized by what we know intellectually about another being, but by an immediate embodied sensation of knowing and being known, a reciprocity in perception. This can only occur here in this very moment; the expression of real relationship is spontaneous and emergent, never standing still. Bathing in the river of time, it is as if our bodies are

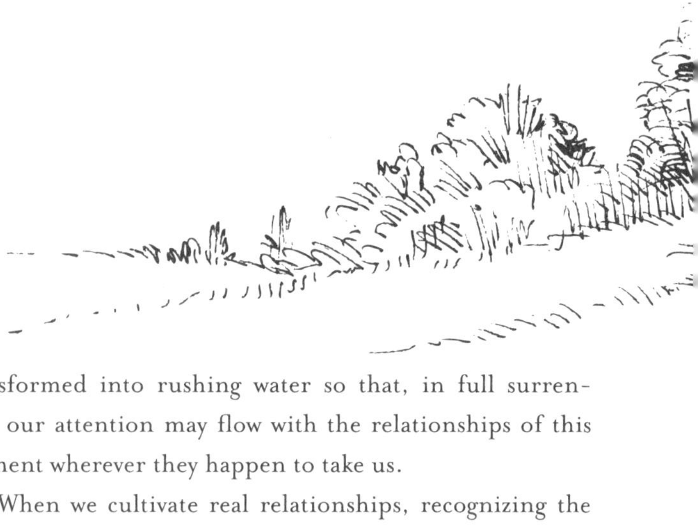

transformed into rushing water so that, in full surrender, our attention may flow with the relationships of this moment wherever they happen to take us.

When we cultivate real relationships, recognizing the intelligence, autonomy, and dignity of other beings, we begin to weave a new story of ourselves. As our relationships deepen, it is as if the lines between ourselves and the world around us begin to blur. As we become more aware that we are nature, we move toward a sense of *interbeing*,

further challenging our notions of separateness. Digging beneath the ego stories of who we think we are, we discover a deeper part of our identity, what we might call our *ecological identity*.

Our ecological identity not only helps us understand what we are, but also helps us understand that this identity is never "ours" alone. This identity exists *intersubjectively*, bound to our real relationships in the world. In simpler terms, when we become aware that we are nature, we also become aware that we are more than just our egoic selves, our names and titles and vocation and beliefs. Beneath all of that, we are more like a living, breathing, changing, relating ecosystem that reaches far beyond the boundaries of our own skin. We are the air we breathe, the water that runs in our veins, the colonies of microbes in our guts, our muscles and bones and our beating hearts, the energy that runs through our nervous system, and the beings with whom we spend our lives. The world lives within us as much as we live within it.

It is even possible that while Forest Bathing, we can experience moments of complete oneness, moments when we let go of the idea of separateness entirely. These moments are not necessarily the goal of the practice, but they are a powerful expression of what is possible. It is wise not to seek these moments. They cannot be forced, and they arise most often when we become skilled at complete relaxation, when we truly let go of our ego stories and have nothing to prove or strive for. In my experience, moments of real oneness come on like an unexpected flash of lightning. It's not something you achieve because you desired it to happen; it happens when you let go of needing anything to happen at all and lose yourself in the sensory experience of simply being alive, here in the body, here in this moment.

Ultimately, we can't think our way toward real relationships. We can't hold the world apart from ourselves, evaluating and labeling and categorizing and consuming, and expect any real intimacy. When we hold the world apart from us, knowing it solely through the mind, it is truly as if we are dreaming of the world because we have no direct experience of it. The longer we live holding the world apart from us, the more easily we fool ourselves into thinking that we know it, and the more likely we are to mistake the dream for a true reality. Forest Bathing wakes us up from this dreaming by reminding us how to be here, now, alive and in relationship to the world around us. We wake up simply by remembering what we truly are.

Sit Spot
PROMPT 2

As you sit, invite your senses
to sit with you.
Notice what unfolds around
and within you.

CHAPTER 2

WHY TRY FOREST BATHING?

NATURE IS HEALTH

Forest Bathing is healthy, plain and simple. You don't need a prescription and you don't need a doctor's supervision. There are no negative side effects, and there's no way to overdose. It's pretty intuitive, really. Nature is good for us. Relaxation is good for us. Giving our brains a break from thinking is good for us.

Being in nature both facilitates and accelerates the body's innate ability to heal itself. It is incredible that the connection between human health and nature is so deep that even the mere sight of a tree can trigger self-healing in humans! This is perhaps why so many people are remembering that time spent in nature is not just recreation, it is also restorative and preventative medicine.

It shouldn't surprise anyone that the human species, which has lived outside for 99.99 percent of its evolutionary history, would be adapted to thrive in the presence of nature. The ever-expanding body of research on this topic suggests that nature reduces symptoms of psychological and physiological stress, balances the nervous system, improves respiratory and cardiovascular functions, restores cognitive abilities, and accelerates attention fatigue recovery.[1] Borrowing from our intellectual understanding of nature, we see that nature is designed for, and thrives on, biodiversity. In any ecosystem, species do not thrive on their own; they depend on each other for their health, reproduction, and defense. And human beings, as nature, have a place at the table, even though we may have forgotten it.

Our bodies, like all life-forms, are designed to stay healthy by being in right relationship with other beings. The oxygen we need to live, for example, comes in part from trees, while the carbon dioxide we exhale sustains trees in return. Beyond the immediate health benefits of oxygen, the absorption and sequestration of carbon by trees and other plants help maintain our atmosphere, without which, we would surely perish.

1. Research studies referenced in this section are found in "Shinrin-Yoku (Forest Bathing) and Nature Therapy: A State-of-the-Art Review," by Margaret M. Hansen, Reo Jones, and Kirsten Tocchini. Published in *International Journal of Environmental Research and Public Health* (August 2017).

But the health benefits we receive from trees go far beyond our need for oxygen. Our immune system, which defends our bodies against disease, is also fortified in the presence of trees.

Japanese researchers believe that this boost in immune function is triggered when we inhale certain organic compounds, known as phytoncides, which are diffused into the air by trees to maintain their own health. When we inhale these compounds, our bodies do something quite incredible: They produce a special white blood cell called a natural killer (NK) cell. NK cells are part of our innate immune system, which means they are not looking for specific diseases; rather, they are hunting down stressed cellular growth, which could become cancerous, and preventatively terminating those cells. Additionally, research has shown that along with NK cell production, Forest Bathing also increases the production of anticancer proteins and decreases the production of stress hormones. This is something quite miraculous! Our bodies, in relationship with trees, activate the self-healing potential of our own nature. Forest Bathing is not a cure for cancer, but it *is* a powerful preventative and adjunctive therapy.

It is not only trees that offer health benefits. Emerging research suggests there are powerful health benefits associated with being near water and engaging with soils; one study even posits that seeing real flowers triggers relaxation in humans.

While it is beyond the scope of this book to fully unpack all the emerging research on this topic, suffice it to say that these "discoveries" are prime examples of ancient knowledge being validated by modern science. For thousands of years, nature was our only physician. It was not until very recently that we began to lose touch with how nature bolsters our natural resilience and improves our overall health. There's nothing complicated about it. Want to be healthier? Simply go sit under a tree and relax.

Rest and Digest

Forest Bathing maximizes the healing benefits of nature not simply because it takes place outside; the real secret is in its slow and restful pace. This slowness activates a shift in the nervous system that promotes self-healing through what is known as the body's "rest and digest" mode. In this mode, our bodies activate self-healing mechanisms that repair, restore, and fortify, but we cannot consciously force the body to do this with our minds. We actually have to slow down and relax.

The self-healing functions of this rest and digest mode are controlled by our parasympathetic nervous system, which is half of our autonomic nervous system. The autonomic nervous system controls all the things your body does without your having to think about it, such as respiration, blood pressure, and organ functions. The body knows how important these functions are, and so your mind cannot override them. We can't, for example, stop our hearts from beating or force our pupils to dilate. Likewise, we can't force our bodies to heal themselves just by thinking about it or wishing it would happen.

You may have heard of the other half of the autonomic nervous system: the sympathetic nervous system. This is what sends people into "fight, flight, freeze, or fawn" mode, which takes over the body in response to a perceived threat. When our sympathetic nervous system is activated, our bodies redirect energy toward the production of stress hormones that will increase respiration, blood pressure, and adrenaline levels. This is the body's way of protecting us when there is immediate danger. Whenever there is a threat, our bodies know we should not be resting and digesting; we should be getting ready to do whatever we need to do to survive. But for what is gained, something is lost as well. When the body is experiencing an involuntary stress response, the brain is not very concerned with cultivating relationships or learning new things, and it is also unable to restore its physical strength.

When we rest, our bodies get to work mending themselves in three important ways. The first is by absorbing nutrients through digestion, giving our bodies what they need to grow, repair damage, and create energy. When we are stressed, our bodies will not gain much from eating even the healthiest foods because nothing is absorbed;

consequently, rest is essential for good nutrition. The second way that rest heals us is by allowing our organs to process and eliminate waste in the form of toxins. Without proper rest, toxins build up in the body and can become dangerous. The third way that rest heals us is by giving our muscles the opportunity to relax and release tension, thus allowing for muscular regeneration; without this regeneration, exercise that would otherwise be healthy can become counterproductive.

So much of our modern health crisis stems from something so perplexingly simple: We have forgotten how to slow down and rest. We are generally overexposed, over-scheduled, overworked, chronically busy people, and we exist in a state of stress almost all the time. Our bodies are simply not evolved to live in constant stress. We can be doing everything else right in taking care of ourselves, but if we do not give ourselves rest and relaxation, it doesn't really matter what we eat or how much we exercise. Ultimately, any health practice that does not include deep rest is unsustainable because our bodies are nature and the pace of nature is dynamic, sometimes moving quickly and sometimes slowly, but never maintaining a breakneck speed for long periods.

Forest Bathing, in inviting us to do very little, is actually giving us permission to do something incredibly healing. Spending time in the nervous system of rest can be strange at first; we're so used to the excitement of our fast-paced world that we can feel a little odd when we begin to slow down. Thankfully, the body is also made for equilibrium; it wants to rest and can remember how if we allow it.

Mental Health

As nature heals the body, it also heals the mind. Our minds are like our bodies in that they do not have infinite quantities of energy. One might even say that the mind also needs to "rest and digest"; it cannot focus or absorb information all the time. Today we live in a mind-driven culture, constantly plugged into a never-ending stream of information and addicted to the speed of modern technology. We don't allow our minds to rest and therefore we experience depression, anxiety, and mental exhaustion that lead to a lack of creativity and emotional well-being.

Just as our bodies have evolved to be in relationship with the beings of the earth, our minds have become attuned to the pace of the natural world. Our minds are like nature. They are dynamic. Sometimes they move fast and sometimes slow, but they are certainly not meant to be racing all the time. Forest Bathing redirects our attention away from our thoughts and toward the sensations of the body, a process which in turn slows down the mind by decreasing rumination and providing mental space to relax and restore.

Today, many people struggle to calm their minds because they have become addicted to mental stimulation. They have forgotten how to relax, how to let go of thinking, how to experience themselves and the world without the distraction of the mind's constant commentary. When they want to calm down, they think about relaxation but do not experience it; they imagine what it would be like, but they do not embody it.

Forest Bathing calms the mind by connecting our bodies to an experience of aliveness that does not require much thought at all. We don't have to think too much about how to enjoy the sight of the sunset or the feeling of the waves touching our toes. We don't have to think about the sound of the wind moving through the canopy or the scent of a wildflower. These simple experiences release us from our addiction to our own thoughts by guiding us toward a sense of deep presence where no thoughts are necessary. For many people today, the rapid pace of life makes such an experience elusive, but with the support of nature, what was impossible becomes easy.

Relational Health

Health does not occur in isolation, but rather in a network of relationships. We receive our health from nature because we are nature. In reciprocity, we can offer health back to nature. This is called *relational health*: the strength of relationship between people and the environments they live in. Relational health is not what you *think* about nature; it is the quality of love and tenderness that informs your actions with nature. In this way, Forest Bathing is not about extracting human wellness from nature; it is a pathway to remembering how to cultivate real relationships with nature so that nature, too, can heal. This reciprocity in health brings us closer to the reality of our interconnectedness and works to dispel the myth of separation.

We cannot heal nature solely through changes in policy or behaviors; to truly heal nature, we must have a fundamental change in our perception. Until we can actually love nature, we cannot *heal* it; we can only attempt to *fix* it. So long as we see the earth, the beings of nature, and our own bodies as mere things, without intelligence, autonomy, or dignity, we can only approach them like machines; they either work or they don't, in which case they need to be fixed. But "fixing" presupposes a dangerous idea of normativity; it suggests that there is a "right" way to exist, and that to be any other way is a problem. Healing, on the other hand, is about recognizing the fullness and dynamic complexity of each being and creating the possibility for what is considered problematic to resolve itself, in its own ways.

We often look around at the land we live upon and think about fixing it, often identifying so-called problems according to our desires for what nature should be, and not according to the way that nature understands itself. In reality, these "problems" are most often nothing more than aesthetic inconveniences to us and have nothing to do with how nature actually works. When the leaves fall, we rake them up, thinking we've fixed a problem when really we've swept away an entire ecosystem that would otherwise have contributed to the health of many plants and animals. When certain plants that we call weeds come, we pull them out, never questioning whether those plants might yield sources of food for other living beings. When plants and animals die, we remove them from sight, never questioning whether their decomposition feeds new and emergent life. We don't often question the ways we tend the land because we preference our aesthetic experience over the living reality of the ecosystem. Oftentimes, what is most beneficial for the land is to simply leave it alone. Nature never needed us in the first place.

This is absolutely not to say that there aren't healthy ways for humans to tend the land. Many Indigenous people have done this historically and still do this today; by knowing the land intimately, what it desires and how it lives, they know how to tend the land in regenerative ways that benefit both humans and the wider ecological community of beings. It is even possible that the vast majority of the earth was once tended by humans in this way. If this is true, it suggests that perhaps our first human ancestors grew to play a very specific ecological role: Perhaps they helped maintain ecological balance and health by supporting all other beings in their development. Perhaps this is our true identity? Perhaps we evolved to be humble servants of the earth, not its master or manager?

Restoring this kind of relationship requires us to actually listen, actually pay attention to the land and how it lives. It requires us to see beyond our own ego-centric preferences for the land, and to recognize that it has its own ways. When we act in concert with nature, we can promote the health of the earth. When we work against nature, we cannot. When we support our planet, we are not managing the land according to our own desires; we are facilitating the life cycles of other living beings, all of whom are interconnected. It is beyond the scope of this book to unpack the ways in which we might reorient our actions toward truly regenerative and sustainable eco-practices, but no greater change is possible unless we first change our perception of nature and correct our fundamentally flawed notion of separateness. This is why Forest Bathing is not overtly concerned with changing actions, but rather with changing perceptions through direct experiences of being nature. It is a practice of subjective activism, a restoration of our own hearts.

When we learn to see nature as something more than a problem to be fixed, we recognize that we are not entitled to speak for the land. We move beyond our judgments of what constitutes "good" nature, and toward an unconditional love. This kind of love does not demand perfection according to our own definitions but instead welcomes the land in full acceptance, even when it is scarred, even when it is not "beautiful," even when it is dying and cycling into newness. As we cultivate relational health, we learn to see the beauty in the wounds of the world and we begin to love it as it is instead of asking it to change for us. If we do seek to change the land, we approach it from a place of humility, knowing that we are tasked to support the life of other beings, and that they in turn support us. As we spend time with the land in this way, we will begin to tend it compassionately and lovingly because our motivations will be selfless and informed by our own experience of being nature. It all begins with this shift in perception.

As you practice Forest Bathing, you might notice that you start relating to the world differently. Over time, the land might seem more like a friend, and you might start tending it differently, too. As you begin to notice how the land lives, perhaps you will let go of your aesthetic preferences and begin to work in harmony with what the land actually wants. Little changes in perception can lead to big changes in our behaviors. Of course, this isn't to say that everyone needs to turn into Captain Planet overnight; everyone is on their own journey, in their own relationships. It's OK to start small. The expression of relational health doesn't have to look any particular way, and we will all find our own path if we commit to simply being in real relationships. At the end of the day, this is about figuring out how to live well, together with all beings. As with any relationship, the journey is the destination.

Sit Spot

PROMPT 3

As you sit, invite curiosity to sit with you.
Notice what unfolds around and within you.

CHAPTER 3

WHY IS FOREST BATHING RELEVANT TODAY?

At the core of all our modern problems, there is a fundamental flaw in our perception of reality. We tend to see the world through the lens of our own human specialness, as though we were not like the rest of nature. In demanding this specialness, we reject our interconnectedness with other living beings, and we ultimately reject ourselves. Our sense of separateness is buttressed by our preference for abstraction over direct experience and our stubborn attachment to our species' prominence, a phenomenon known as anthropocentrism.

All these factors point to the crux of the modern problem: We have forgotten how to simply be what we are by authentically participating in the sensory realms of nature.

We are so distracted by our specialness, our thoughts, and our desire for instant gratification that we have lost touch with how to just be here, how to bathe in the river of time. When we remember that we are nature, and that nature yearns to live in relationship, we wake up from our trance of separateness; this awakening is really the essence of Forest Bathing. When we experience ourselves as nature, we instantly become attuned to the experience of aliveness that is shared by all other beings. It is simply waiting for us to pay attention and wake up.

Abstraction

All relationships begin with the senses. It's how our brains, during infancy, learn what relationships mean in an embodied way. To unpack this, let's do a quick thought experiment. Picture someone you love—maybe a parent or sibling or friend or partner—but imagine that you've never actually met them. You've never felt their embrace or heard the sound of their voice or looked into their eyes. All you have is a book with all the information about that person, every fact there is to know. Can you imagine what that kind of relationship would feel like?

Most people say that it would be difficult to fall in love based solely on the facts; the *idea* or *abstraction* of a person isn't a satisfactory substitute for the physical human being. This makes sense because love is not abstract. Love is felt directly, in the moment and in our bodies. Talking about love and actually experiencing it are in no way comparable because our emotions are somatic, not intellectual. Over time, we may fall in love with our ideas about people, but there can be no real love without the sensing body.

Relationship is an experience of not being alone, of intimately knowing and vulnerably being known in such a way that lines of separation start to blur. We feel love when we are in relationship because we crave authentic intimacy. What we experience as love is really the body saying, "I value this intimacy, and I am willing to nurture this relationship so that I do not lose it." This feeling is what prompts us to behave in ways that benefit the health of a *relationship*. Abstraction denies us the opportunity of intimacy, and therefore love, because it holds people at a distance and reduces them to mere facts.

We unconsciously favor abstraction over direct experience for two reasons: first, because it is quicker and seems more efficient; and second, because it allows us to sidestep our own vulnerability. Abstraction appears more efficient because it allows us to assume that we already know what things are like. When we rely on abstraction, we don't have to exercise any genuine curiosity, and we don't have to spend time performing our own investigation. While we sometimes take the abstraction shortcut with people, we almost always take it with nature. We see a tree and immediately our attention moves to categorize it by species, size, shape, and location; we then believe we have "known" it, and we move on. But we have not known it at all, or our knowledge exists only in abstract terms. In our haste to know, we've simply collected some data so that we have a story about "that big round maple tree in the park." But we never really saw the beauty of this tree because we relied on abstract ideas instead of direct experience.

If we had actually stopped and sat with that tree, what would we have noticed? By experiencing it with all our senses, what depth of relationship could we have cultivated? Because we are so skilled at convincing ourselves that we already know what things are like, we can be genuinely surprised when we realize the potential depth and complexity of our sensory experiences and resultant relationships. The life of every single being is unique; it is not just "that big round maple tree in the park." It has a story that you will never know until you take the time to actually be with it, to intimately know it beyond broad categories and generalized facts.

In order to engage with our fellow beings in this way, we must be vulnerable enough to be intimate. Whereas abstraction objectifies things so that you come to know them in a detached way, direct experience allows two subjects to know each other more intimately. For many people, this can be intimidating because we are often terrified of being known, of being seen for what we are, and yet there is no other path to relationship; intimacy and immediacy are prerequisites to the experience of love. This is as true in human relationships as it is with those in the more than human world.

When we rely on abstractions, we cannot see the dynamic quality of things, nor can we see their ephemeral and unique inner beauty. Abstraction demands an unnatural sense of separation. When we view the big round maple in the park, where does our consideration stop? Does it include the soils, the water, the insects and birds who live in the tree? Does it include the seed that formed the tree, or the decay that will eventually return it to the earth? If we rely on abstraction, we see a fixed, discrete object, separated from all its relationships; if we rely on direct experience, we see that there is much more to the big round maple than we initially thought: It is a living, thriving, dynamic ecosystem. Once we recognize what we are actually seeing, we are prepared to participate in that ecosystem through embodied relationship. Facts—categories and abstract ideas—are what hold us apart from the world and cause us to reject the kind of intimacy that results in knowing and being known by nature.

We tend to think of ourselves abstractly for a similar reason: because it is easier and seemingly more efficient to describe ourselves through ideas than it is to understand ourselves as evolving, emergent, natural beings. We also tend to enjoy thinking about ourselves abstractly because it gives us the illusion of specialness and separateness. We like our labels—the ideas that we use to define ourselves—because we think there is great merit in being someone special. We cling to the abstract stories that separate us from others and the world because we think they are what makes us worthy of love. At the end of the day, most of our self-reflection is based on defining *who* we are, but very rarely do we ever inquire seriously into the dynamic experience of *what* we are, here and now. Perhaps this is because what we are is not so special; what we are, in all its elegant simplicity, is nature, and we are truly not separate at all.

When we arrive in nature, we do not need an abstract identity, a story about who we are. In the eyes of the forest, we are all human beings, without distinctions based on culture, religion, gender, class, politics, occupations, interests, surnames, or any other identifying category or label. The forest doesn't perceive us as special in any way and therefore receives us in our most vulnerable and complete authenticity, inviting us to be exactly what we are: living, breathing, moving nature—nothing more and nothing less. This experience liberates us from the stories that limit us and allows us to know our true nature.

When we let go of the need for abstraction, we can experience both ourselves and the beings of nature as they truly are: interconnected in the river of time. We do not come with preformed assumptions or labels, but rather with a genuine curiosity, vulnerability, and openness to experience the world anew in each and every moment. Accessing this openness is challenging at first because we have been taught that knowledge anchors our reality, when in fact knowledge prevents us from approaching the world with the intelligence of our hearts. Through direct experience, we push past abstraction and discover our deepest, most interconnected self.

Bodylessness

How did we become so numb that we no longer appreciate the experience of simply being alive and being present in the world in this moment? Being present begins within us, in our perception of our own bodies. We cannot think our way to feeling alive or to experiencing real relationship. Our minds can only imagine what aliveness would feel like or remember what it felt like in the past. It is the body that connects us to the present because it is our bodies that can bathe in the river of time. How do you experience the immediacy of this moment without the sensing body? How do you experience the sensation of wind on your bare skin, observe a sunset, take a breath, or fall in love without the body?

We are not taught to perceive of ourselves as bodies; we tend to think of our "self" as our ideas, thoughts, opinions, and stories. Consequently, we think of our bodies as something more like vehicles or houses for our consciousness, that which we call our "self." By identifying with our thoughts and not our bodies, we ontologically reduce our bodies to something like a machine—something to be optimized, fixed, and maintained, but not something to be experienced or loved. As our emotions are somatic, such reduction also negates the importance of our emotional bodies in deference to the reductive certainty of our thinking minds. The body, however, is not a machine, nor is it something that we "have." The body is the experience of ourselves as nature, but because we do not identify with it, we have become numb and bodyless.

When we are born, we experience reality primarily through the body. When we are young, we move, we play, we have an intense sensory curiosity for the world, and our bodies are the central influencers in our perception of reality. Our early somatic memories inform us how to build relationships by creating associations between sensory experiences and emotional states. This is not exclusive to human relations, but rather applies to our relations with everything around us. This is why young children are masters at Forest Bathing; they do it reflexively and naturally.

The social push toward bodylessness begins early in our development. Oftentimes, learning to ignore the body is first taught at school and is part of a widespread primal wounding. Children are expected to sit for long hours in stillness and silence with their attention focused on whatever they are told to do. They are expected to eat, use the bathroom, and rest at specific times, regardless of whether they need to or not. In short, children are not educated to be attuned to the needs of their bodies but are instead taught to ignore and suppress them. Despite the fact that bodies are diverse and have different needs, everyone is made to follow the same schedule for physical self-care; this downplays the individualized experience of the body in deference to a one-size-fits-all approach. To compound the lack of attention on bodily self-care, the emphasis on cognitive learning in early education minimizes the importance of sensory development and often leads to children's senses being underutilized and underdeveloped.

By the time we're adults, we don't remember how to pay attention to the body anymore, and we think we know what everything feels like anyway. We don't even hold any curiosity about the texture of a rose petal or the visual details of the trees outside our windows. We rush through sensory experiences, eating our food, for example, so quickly that we barely taste anything. Research shows that many people are only aware of their bodies during three experiences: sex, exercise, and pain. We become addicted to the never-ending stream of information we receive through screens or social engagement, and even when we reach unsustainable levels of information overload, we just can't seem to stop ourselves from consuming more and more and more. We numb ourselves further with drugs, alcohol, and all other sorts of anesthetics just to keep up with the pace of our hectic lives. And we end up feeling almost nothing at all.

In our numbness, we tend to objectify our own bodies, further validating our bodylessness. As an object, the body loses all dignity, authority, and wisdom of its own. The body becomes a mere project. We say "Treat your body like a temple," but our bodies have much more in common with living forests than inanimate temples. Like forests, our bodies do not need to be tamed. We judge our bodies ugly or flawed and so we rush around trying to fix them or improve them without ever asking ourselves, *What could be more beautiful than a living forest?* If we do not feel alive in our bodies, then how can we ever learn to love the nature of ourselves?

When we begin to perceive that our bodies are alive and are not mere objects, then we have taken the first step toward having a relationship with nature. This is about breaking down the illusion of separation. We cannot participate in the aliveness of nature if we do not perceive of our bodies as being interconnected with it. To love nature, to form a real relationship, we must begin with the nature inside.

Anthropocentrism

There's a strong bias in our culture which suggests that human beings are somehow special in contrast to other beings. We privilege our humanness over all other life, creating a hierarchy of ontological value. Because of this, we have a hard time wrestling with the idea that the earth, and the beings and phenomenon of nature, have their own intelligence, wisdom, and cultures. We are taught to believe that the world of nature unfolds mathematically like a machine, while humans, who are not nature, have free will guided by thought and knowledge. This is perhaps the height of our hubris: We do not affiliate or identify ourselves with all other life, and we see our intelligence as somehow more valid than that of all other beings. And in our specialness, we have made ourselves lonely by rejecting the community of nature. In an interconnected world, we have chosen to be isolated.

The culture of anthropocentrism extends bodylessness beyond humans; it projects our bias about the value and dignity of our own bodies onto the body of the earth and the bodies of other beings. We don't perceive of the earth as a living body. We ignore it, or else we view it as a project or something to be optimized. We do this to smaller environments as well, even those as small as our backyards; we don't see the inner beauty of the land we live upon because we don't know how to see it. And yet it is nature, both within and beyond us, that can help us remember how to participate in the experience of being alive. Nature can teach us to see with new eyes. It can revitalize our relationships.

Recognizing the autonomy, intelligence, and dignity of nature helps us to dissolve the sense that we, as humans, are special and separate. We come to understand that we are not exempt from the responsibilities of our relationships, and we feel called upon to live in better relationship with our fellow beings. When we release ourselves from the illusion of anthropocentrism, we become able to genuinely care for the land because we sense that it is alive and that it can suffer, just like us. It is from this depth of relationship and shift in perception that true compassion is exercised. If we are only caring for the land out of

obligation while continuing to believe in our specialness, then our compassion is little more than a performance.

When we abandon our anthropocentric bias, we face the challenging reality of what it means to be nature: We live and die just like everything else, and the world does not revolve around our desires or our attachment to the concept of permanence. So much of our denial about what we are may be rooted in the fear that, individually and collectively, we are as fragile as any other being that lives on this earth. We desperately want to be special because we don't want to face this aspect of our existence. But when we do confront our impermanence, and the impermanence of the world, we may also encounter immense gratitude.

Understanding our own fragility helps us recognize that we are not needed here, not in the absolute sense. We're not ultimately here to manage or save or control the emergent ecological phenomenon that is life on Earth. When we realize this, perhaps we can also take a breath in relief and realize how incredibly lucky we are simply to be here? When we relate to the world with our heart, with real love, and not with the fears of our minds, perhaps we can stop worrying so much and experience a gratitude for the life that is here with us? Perhaps we might understand that we are not alone and that we are always going to be one with this place somehow, in some form, not in abstract terms, not in thoughts or opinions, but as the flesh of the earth, as the miracle of life itself?

Moving toward Real Relationships

At its core, the modern problem is one of mistaken identity. In our hubris, we have forgotten that we are the land, that our bodies are nature. We must remember how to participate in nature not at the level of thought, but in the shared experience of being alive through our senses. As we share our sensations with other beings, we begin to cultivate real relationships over time. These relationships reveal to us the inner beauty of beings. They galvanize sustainable and regenerative action. When we cultivate this kind of authentic relationship, we know what we truly are, and we know how to listen and bear witness; we do not need to be judgmental and coercive toward ourselves, others, and the more than human world.

In attempts to escape numbness, loneliness, and abstraction, people try all sorts of things; they fill their time looking for the meaning of life, training their minds to become introspective, or studying the wisdom of someone else's story. They do all this when so much of what they are looking for is right under their feet, in the air they breathe, and within their own bodies. The mind will not resolve our isolation; we will never feel less lonely by spending more time with only the idea of ourselves. But the world is waiting patiently for us to return, and when we let go of our "self," we are never truly alone.

Forest Bathing is about remembering we are nature. It's so simple that it almost seems silly, maybe even embarrassingly so at first. It's challenging to grapple with the idea that something as easy as sitting under a tree or feeling the grass under our toes or listening to a chorus of the birds or gazing at a cloud has the power to so profoundly change our perception. We cannot override our sense of separation with thoughts; we cannot realize we are nature by thinking about it. The shift in our perception happens slowly and organically as we dwell within these sensory relationships, as we come to know the world intimately and are vulnerable enough to allow the beings of the world to know us.

As we spend more time in these relationships, we cannot help but begin to perceive the world not as a set of objects that we hold apart from ourselves, but rather as an intersubjective and participatory experience of aliveness and sensory communication that moves in every direction, relating all beings to each other. In this way, we are learning to experience nature as nature experiences itself, and this is precisely what we have lost in our modern lives. We are tasked to remember that it is our relationships that truly define us; this is the ancient wisdom that every other being knows and we have forgotten. This is the wisdom we need to remember today.

Sit Spot
PROMPT 4

As you sit, invite your heart
to sit with you.
Notice what unfolds around
and within you.

Chapter 4

HOW DOES FOREST BATHING WORK?

Embodiment

Forest Bathing begins by shifting our conscious attention away from the thinking mind and toward the sensing body. If we focus all of our attention on the senses, we will experience what is known as *embodiment*. Embodiment means that we are primarily perceiving of ourselves and the world with our animate, living bodies, and not abstractly through our analytical, discursive minds. When we practice embodiment, we begin to perceive the world and ourselves differently; instead of a static series of objects, we encounter a world that is boundlessly connected through a network of constant communication and interbeing.

If you could see this network with your eyes, it might look like a massive web where every being is connected to all other beings around them through sensory awareness. From bacteria all the way to whales, beings are paying attention to each other in an omnidirectional and multisensory language. They practice relationships through their own embodiment, through the intelligence of the senses that allow them to navigate this world. When we practice embodiment, we also become more aware of our relationships and of how we might participate in them with the intelligence of our bodies and the sensory vocabulary of our nature.

Another way you might think of embodiment is simply as *presence*: the ability to be here now by giving full attention to the sensing body and keeping the mind in check. The mind can imagine the sound of a bell in the future or remember the sound of a bell in the past, but it is the body, and only the body, that hears the sound of the bell ringing here and now. The senses are experiencing reality directly, and so they anchor us in both time and place. They are the gateways to immediacy.

When we are stuck in our thinking minds, our attention is solely on our thoughts. Imagine walking through the forest while chatting with a friend or thinking about work you need to do. How much of the forest would you really notice? Probably not very much. It's not your fault, it's just the way our brains work. If we are placing attention upon our thoughts, our brains cannot also process the sensory information they are receiving from the world and bring it to our conscious attention. Our attention is like a spotlight in the vast darkness of our entire conscious experience; the light shines on one thing at a time, and the rest is obscured. In other words, because the mind only has so much attention to give, we cannot be focused on all things at once.

When we are not paying attention to the sensing body, the world around us becomes little more than an obstacle course. You can be deep in your thoughts and still walk through the forest and not run into a tree. This is because your brain is still feeding the general impression of the physical world to your conscious attention. What you are missing is the details. To your brain, which is designed to conserve energy by screening how much sensory information is truly essential to process, there is no reason to show you the intricate fractal patterns of the flowers at your feet, or the delicate scent of the pines wafting in the air, or the sound of the leaves rustling above your head. To the thinking mind, these are trivial details, unworthy of your conscious attention.

When you move through the world without paying attention to your senses, your brain simply categorizes the objects around you in a superficial way. Your mind says something like, "That's a tree. That's another tree. That's a squirrel. That's a tree..." and you walk right by without

a second thought, unconsciously satisfied with this cursory interaction. In the moment, you don't realize how much you have missed; you probably don't even consider it. And if you are staring at your phone while you walk, then you might not even recognize that there are trees around you; you might not be aware of anything more than the terrain beneath your feet. In those moments of true distraction, our brains put such a heavy filter on incoming sensory information that only really strong phenomena, like a car horn, can break through to our conscious attention. Even if we direct all our attention to the mind, the body still has emergency protocols designed to wake us up to being here when our survival is at stake.

In Forest Bathing, we recognize that the details of the world are essential for cultivating real relationships. Whether the relationship is with a single being or the totality of nature, our sensing bodies are the medium through which nature relates to us and through which we relate to nature. There truly is reciprocity here; beings like animals and plants have their own sensory ability to know you as a physical being; they know whether you are safe or dangerous, and whether you might somehow connect with them in relationship. The world is not indifferent to your physical presence, though it is indifferent to your thoughts and opinions.

In embodiment, we practice both our ability to know and our ability to recognize how we may be known. It all happens at the level of *sensory phenomena*: the sounds, sights, smells, tastes, and sensations of the body that yield direct experiences where two or more subjects meet in time and space. As we become more practiced in embodiment and our sensory abilities become more interconnected, we may even begin to experience various levels of synesthesia. And though we are not able to directly experience the sensory abilities of other beings, we may, if we pay close enough attention, begin to understand and appreciate them.

When we awaken the intelligence of our sensing bodies, we also reanimate the natural wisdom of our emotional bodies. As we have discussed, our emotions are somatic: They are directly tied to our physical experiences. So, when we begin to feel at a sensory level, we simultaneously begin to feel at an emotional level. All of the emotional states we experience in relationship work to cultivate deeper levels of intimacy. Whether it is pleasure, catharsis, joy, grief, mirth, or even pain, these experiences bring us closer to our own nature, our own ecological authenticity. In a culture that has denigrated both the physical and emotional bodies, reclaiming our emotional states in embodiment is an act of resilience.

When you offer your attention to the experiences of the body, it becomes much more difficult to generalize the world around you. You become aware that no two things in nature are identical. No two trees, no two stones, no two birds. Paying attention to our senses reveals that every being, including you, has a unique elegance and inner beauty that can only be witnessed in real relationship. We enter a relationship with nature by recognizing that the world around us is not mechanistic and mass-produced, nor is it merely the setting for our human story; it is living and dying and changing, and we are just one character in its much grander mythology. In Forest Bathing, we are invited to participate in the nature and mythology of this moment, provided we stop thinking our way past it.

Slowing Down

Experiencing embodiment requires us to slow down. We simply can't pay attention to our senses when we're rushing. Furthermore, our senses become much stronger and much more complex when we slow down and allow ourselves to fully experience them. Many people notice this when they practice what is called *mindful eating*. Try this sometime: Eat something very slowly, with your full attention on the sensory experience of eating. Notice the textures, temperature, flavors, sounds, and all the sensations that arise as you chew and swallow. Also notice how you feel as you eat, what

the emotional experience of being in relationship with your food is like. You may find that, unlike the rapidity of our cognitive communication, the sensory language of nature becomes more evocative as it becomes more intentionally slow and deliberate. Each sensation contains an incredible richness, and as we take time to experience these sensations fully, we become more aware of how much we are missing in our normal hastiness.

Slowing down can be a real challenge; we spend most of our lives rushing about, believing that time is slipping away and that there is never enough of it. In response to this anxiety, we tend to move even faster, hoping that we might catch our breath once we "get ahead." Of course, we rarely ever do get ahead; instead, we become accustomed to our busyness, justifying it as the normal way of things, mistakenly telling ourselves that the world simply moves quickly, when really the pace of our lives is up to us.

In nature, nothing is rushed. As we remember this and begin to slow ourselves down, it can at first appear that the entire world is slowing down with us. It can feel as though each moment is elongating, yielding to our embodied attention. When we slow our bodies down, our minds follow suit, and so this slowness serves to maintain our awareness of embodiment. The thing that might be most helpful to remember is that the destination is here, no matter where you are. In any small area, there are a million sensations to experience. When we slow down and pay attention, we begin to notice this wealth of sensory phenomena. So, it's not about getting to the top of the mountain or all the way to the waterfall; it's about being right here, recognizing that in each step there is something as gratifying as anything we have yet to encounter. When we relax into slowness, we're simply giving ourselves permission to be present.

As we slow down, we begin to experience a state which might be called *timelessness*; this is the antidote to our panicked anxiety about time. When we give ourselves permission to slow down, without any goals or agenda, we suddenly experience an abundance of time. This can feel awkward at first because we are so conditioned to think of time as a scarce resource that must be maximized by rushing about. But then, as we relax into it, we come to realize that rushing about is in fact a counterproductive distraction. When we slow down, we cease to think of this moment as a resource and begin to recognize it as our home.

Practicing embodiment and slowness allows us the time to relate with beings and places in new ways. Even places you are familiar with may reveal new aspects of themselves. Things that have gone unnoticed for years might suddenly captivate your attention. You'll find yourself scratching your head and saying, "Was this *always* here?" It could be anything, really: a tiny mushroom hidden by fallen leaves, the intricate details in a frothy wave receding upon the sand, or the delicate notes of a birdsong. It is not simply a question of noticing these often overlooked things, but rather of recognizing how vivid and life-affirming they can be when we take the time to fully experience them. Sensations that we often rush through such as the scent of flowers, the feeling of grass on our toes, or a sudden gust of wind become unexpectedly invigorating when we actually savor what they feel like in the body.

The Imaginal Sense

As you remember how to relax your mind and offer your attention to nature, you might notice that you are also remembering how to experience the world through what is called the *imaginal sense*, or the inner knowing of the heart. We all have imaginal experiences, but most of us have been conditioned to write them off as "imaginary."

The distinction between imaginal and imaginary is that imaginary phenomena are what we *actively create* using our imaginations, whereas imaginal phenomena are what we *spontaneously receive* through our imaginations.

The imaginal can be described as a sort of reverie or daydream that comes over us when we slow down our thinking minds. When we experience the imaginal, we are not actively steering our imaginations, but rather gently allowing the moment to embody an imagery that it desires. This is not something that we do by focusing; instead, such imagery organically arises when we simply relax our minds, slow down, and live in our bodies. Perhaps the imaginal sense is how we perceive the dreams of the earth; these dreams do not originate within us but instead move through us, connecting us to what is mysterious and unexplainable. Or perhaps it is more like we encounter the nature of our unconscious, which is linked to the unconscious of the entire world.

One common way the imaginal shows up is through what we might call *impressions* from the realms of nature, both within and beyond our bodies. As we become aware of these impressions, we might feel a deep sense of intuition, or inner knowing. We might also feel a sense that the imaginal relays impressions from other beings to our conscious attention, as though plants and animals were somehow communicating with us. While letting our minds drift into reverie, we create a spaciousness for other voices to enter, and through the imaginal sense, perhaps it is not so impossible to experience the beings of nature offering us something, asking something of us, or simply sharing their stories?

In Forest Bathing, we need not be overly concerned with determining what is imaginal and what is imaginary, but it is important for us to at least be open to the inherent dignity and value of our experiences, no matter how unusual or indescribable they may seem. If we have experiences that we cannot explain, maybe it is because they are not meant to be explained? Maybe we are simply supposed to carry them with us? Perhaps they are part of the language of nature, connecting us to this moment, washing past us in the river of time?

To create space for these experiences, we need to let go of our desire to "figure it out." We don't have to understand what they are, or where they come from, or what they might mean; we only have to offer them hospitality. When we relax into the present moment without the desire to explain everything to ourselves, we stop constraining the imagination and thinking of ourselves as its director. It is as if we are rewilding the imagination, letting it move its own body however it wishes so that we, in turn, might share in its aliveness. This, too, is a relationship—one that we should remember to tend.

The Mirror Effect

When we start to slow down and pay attention, we witness all that unfolds within the world of nature: all the joy, the nourishment, the interconnectedness alongside all the decay, and withering, and death. In observing this, we know that these cycles belong to us as well, that these experiences are our birthright and mirror our participation in a fully interconnected world. Whereas we are taught to suppress what is considered "negative" or "ugly" in our tamed lives, in nature, we acknowledge that there is beauty in every facet of living and dying. Gazing into the mirror of nature is what truly gives us a full picture of who we are.

Once we have learned to see ourselves more completely, we are ready for nature to mentor us in the practice of self-love. As we look deeper, we begin to notice that nature does not hide its imperfections, its brokenness, or its impermanence. Leaves fall, animals die, rivers run dry, and fires leave

their marks upon the land. At first, witnessing all of this can be uncomfortable. We are attached to thinking of nature romantically. We believe that everything should be beautiful all of the time, but then, as we sit with what is real, something shifts within us: We begin to see that nature's imperfections, impermanence, and brokenness are also the sources of its beauty, resilience, and ever-evolving story. When we realize we are nature, we become free to explore our own authentic story in its full complexity and depth.

We live in a culture that strives for permanence, beauty, and perfection in all things. Instead of being content in this moment, just the way we are, we continuously strive to improve ourselves. We tend to see ourselves as gardens in need of sculpting. We spend a lot of time focusing on flaws, and so we are constantly at work trimming and pruning and planting and cutting. We fail to see that imperfections are beautiful because they are authentically part of life. This oversight leads us to work so hard that we never have time to sit, relax, and enjoy the gardens of ourselves. Why do we value perfection at the expense of the present moment?

Perhaps we garden ourselves and the nature around us for the same reason: because we do not have healthy relationships with suffering, illness, and death. We don't like these things in our gardens, in our bodies, or in our stories about ourselves. We don't like getting older or the scars we collect in life, and we don't like it when things fall apart or fail to conform to our most romantic visions of how life ought to be. But this kind of willful self-deception denies that we are nature. Part of Forest Bathing involves reconciling with an unapologetic truth: Suffering, illness, and death coexist within us. This means that our love for our bodies and for the world cannot be conditional; we learn to love nature by seeing the exquisitely vulnerable beauty of things as they are, not as we believe they should be according to some romantic, subjective ideal.

When we understand that we are nature, we begin to see that it's alright to be broken, inconstant, and imperfect because that is how we are meant to be. Both physically and emotionally, we have ups and downs, beginnings and endings, and are forever in flux—just like all other beings. As we become aware of this, we reflexively become more like nature: resilient in the face of inevitable change. The beings of the more than human world mentor us in the practice of life and death. We begin to feel at home within ourselves, no matter where we are in our journey, because we feel that we are not walking alone. And perhaps most amazingly of all, we can find aliveness in our imperfections, our brokenness, and even our last moments in these bodies. As we look deeper into nature, she stares deeper into us, dissolving our sense of separation bit by bit until finally it is gone.

Meeting Our Edges

When we realize we are nature, we encounter the world as it really is, not as we wish it would be. For this reason, our experience of embodied aliveness brings us closer to parts of ourselves, such as our stories and our relationships, that we may find challenging. To be challenged is not a bad thing; challenges simply raise questions about our boundaries, what we are willing to encounter and what we are not. These boundaries represent our *edges*: experiences where we begin to feel uncomfortable.

We all have different edges, just as we all have different lives. Some of us have an edge around experiencing grief, while others have an edge around experiencing joy. Some of us have edges around particular sensory experiences such as textures, sounds, or visuals. There is no edge that must be pushed, but sometimes it is at our edges that we experience aspects of aliveness we would otherwise deny ourselves. If we can summon the courage to exist at that edge and not turn away from the reality of the moment, then we are likely to receive incredible gifts.

Forest Bathing is not exclusively about pleasure, although it often is pleasurable. The practice invites us to live at our edges as a way of deepening our relationship with nature. When we move beyond numbness, we encounter not only a more vivid sensory experience of relationship, but also a more vivid emotional reality. In this way, we are called to practice unconditional love: We are tasked with becoming less judgmental, both outwardly and inwardly, in pursuit of being fully alive and experiencing real—not romantic or idealized—relationship to nature.

Outwardly, we begin to experience the world with less judgment as we lean into our edges. Instead of perceiving something like rain as an inconvenience, we see it as rain, a phenomenon which is quite amazing to feel on our bodies.

Even if you prefer not to get wet, have you ever stopped simply to listen to the rain, or watched with curiosity as it moves upon a glass window? Instead of wishing for silence, we learn to accept the sounds of nature, even when they include the voices of hikers passing by; are they not nature also? We might even start to notice that a tree is still beautiful even after it has stopped living, or that the desiccated blooms of autumn are as elegant as their younger springtime selves. Oftentimes, the edges we have about the world are simply our judgments, but the realms of nature do not abide by our preferences; they simply exist as they are. As we become less judgmental, we begin to see beauty in things we once found unbeautiful.

Inwardly, we learn to regard ourselves with less judgment as well. We become more comfortable with the full range of experiences available to us through the body, including experiences many of us deny ourselves. When we open up in this way, we may discover that emotions often contain their opposites. Boredom becomes a steppingstone to inspiration. Grief becomes a pathway to praise and gratitude. Whether they engender laughter or tears, our inner experiences are real, and they are gifts that we may choose to accept or reject. We need not pathologize our inner experiences. There is nothing wrong with experiencing "negative" emotional states, and there is nothing embarrassing about experiencing strong emotions. Our emotions are a part of our embodiment; they are not simply thoughts. They are the voice of our inner nature.

Whatever edges you encounter, be both gentle and brave in their presence. Your body will guide you. As we cultivate real relationships, we become more willing to experience beings in deeper levels of authenticity. When we are willing to be present, we find that our edges shift over time, and soon we are able to experience more than what we once imagined possible. The process simply requires us to sit with beings as they are, and not as we wish them to be.

There's No Right or Wrong Way

Nature is not a machine; it is emergent and intelligent, always changing, always finding new ways. As nature, we are no different. We're made to experiment. What works for one of us might not work for another. What works for us today might not work tomorrow. There are no consistent answers in Forest Bathing, only questions, curiosities, and explorations. Your body, your inner nature, is on a journey to discover how it relates to the nature all around it. It doesn't matter where you are, or what capabilities your body does or doesn't possess; we just have to be here, now, and let our bodies guide us toward relationship.

Relationships take time, and they can have their ups and downs. As you spend more time practicing Forest Bathing, you'll develop your own ways, and you'll come to know your own edges. Over time, things will shift in your relationship with nature. You won't be consciously aware of this shift, at least not at first. You won't have some grand breakthrough culminating in the ultimate authentic relationship. Change happens slowly and with repetition. That's what makes Forest Bathing a practice.

There is nothing complicated here. You don't have to work hard or have an agenda. You don't need to "know what you're doing," either. In fact, it is actually best when you feel a little bit lost: That's how you know your mind is letting go of the need for things to unfold in a certain way. Instead of seeking what you think you need, be open to receiving what the land has to offer. Just keep remembering to return to the body, return to the present moment, and return to an awareness of relationship through the senses.

If it's hard at first, then try it for only one minute. And then the next time, try it for two minutes. Sometimes we think so much that it can be difficult to come back to the body's direct experience. Sometimes we become numb from overthinking, and then sensory experiences start to feel overwhelming. There's no need to push yourself to do anything before you feel ready. And it's OK to laugh when we find ourselves in awe at the sight of a tiny mushroom that no one else seems to notice; we should never take ourselves too seriously. When in doubt, just sit down somewhere and invite patience to sit with you; let the world teach you what it means to pay attention and how to bathe in the river of time.

Sit Spot
PROMPT 5

As you sit, invite your imagination to sit with you. Notice what unfolds around and within you.

Chapter 5

The Practice in Ten Simple Steps

In this chapter, you will find ten simple steps that you can use solo or with your friends and family. The steps do not specify any amount of time. It is up to you how long you spend on each one, but you should know that nothing in this process is ever enhanced by rushing. After moving through the steps a few times, you may begin to notice that your body has remembered what to do and how to do it.

The ten steps are laid out in a sequence; allow each one to be an *invitation*. Invitations are not assignments or exercises; there's nothing you have to do or not do. Consider accepting these invitations in the spirit of indulging your sense of curiosity. Try not to think about the invitations too much; your mind may not know how to receive them.

Simply allow your body to lead, and let the mind relax. Offer your full attention to your senses and bear witness to the intelligence of your own nature.

Step 1: Choose a place.

Pick a place. Any place. Wherever you are, you can find relationship there, within your body and with everything around it. Let go of dualistic judgments about what is living and what is not, what is natural and what is not, and you will find that the world is a unified field of nature, inviting you to participate in its aliveness. Everywhere you go, the world is populated by beings of nature. They exist in endless forms, including soils, stones, plants, winds, waters, mushrooms, metals, sunlight, clouds, lava, microbes, animals, rainbows, and bolts of lightning. Nothing is excluded; everything participates.

Once we see that there is no separation between humans and nature, we may also begin to recognize that everything we build is nature, even when transformed. This means our houses are nature, our clothes are nature, our food is nature; even jet planes, cell phones, and electricity are transfigurations of nature. Having a relationship with nature is not so much about connecting with a romantic vision of lush "wilderness"; it's about perceiving that the world around you is nature, no matter where you are, and honoring the available relationships, whatever they may be.

You don't have to go far. You can practice Forest Bathing anywhere: in your backyard, a garden, local park, arboretum, or in the depths of the outlands. You can do it in a parking lot with a single tree. In fact, you don't have to rely solely on trees: There's plenty of incredible relationships in the desert, on the beaches, in the tundra, and even in cities. You can even practice Forest Bathing from within your own home! All you need is to be in your body.

It is perhaps best to practice Forest Bathing where you live or spend a lot of time; do it in a place you'll come back to over and over again so that you'll experience the deepening of that relationship over time. After a few years, the place may become like a friend that has seen you get older, too. We can build a relationship with any space; we can see the inner beauty of all places and all beings.

STEP 2: RELEASE JUDGMENT.

Remember that your body already knows how to do this. You aren't learning something new; you're remembering something you were born with but may have forgotten. There is no right or wrong way to have your own personal relationship with nature; your relationship should be, above all else, an authentic expression of how *you* exist in nature and as nature. This is not a performance, so let go of expectations about how it's supposed to look. There are infinite ways to be in relationship, all of them unique to a specific place and a specific moment.

Releasing judgment serves us in two important ways. First, it liberates us from anxiety about whether we are "doing it right." When we focus on doing it right, we are not focused on what is real, what is directly in front of us. When our focus is on doing it right, we live in constant distraction, haunted by the nagging fear that we may be doing it *wrong*.

To achieve full awareness of our embodiment is to live without such worries. When you find yourself struggling

with judgment, simply affirm that you are experiencing what is appropriate for the present moment and know that things will change. We often want to see results immediately, but remember that relationship takes time, and remember that what you are doing is quite simply learning to be, here in your body, here in this moment, here in this nature. The experiences we gather while Forest Bathing will not reveal their full depths right away. Imagine that every moment you share with nature is like planting a seed in your heart: You may not be aware of what is growing within you until days, weeks, months, or even years have passed.

The second way that releasing judgment serves us is by opening up the space we need to fall in love with what is real without demanding revisions and alterations. When we release judgment, we abandon the concept of a "perfect day" or "perfect weather" or "perfect place" for Forest Bathing. We recognize that to truly know a place, and to know ourselves, we must experience it in all weather and in all seasons. We become more interested in the dynamic beauty of the ever-changing world than in crystalizing a memory of "that one perfect moment."

Our attachment to our desires makes releasing judgment difficult. You may think there's some kind of special experience that you're supposed to have while Forest Bathing, like being very calm, or feeling the kind of spiritual connection to nature that you often see dramatized in movies. To let go of these expectations, try to cultivate a sense of *purposelessness*. Learn to carry the story that purposelessness is liberating: It provides the freedom to experience all possibilities. There is no test, there is no correct answer, there is nothing to achieve. Once we learn to embrace purposelessness, the beauty of ordinary things begins to reveal itself, and we relax into presence with fewer internal distractions.

Try to remember that you can't open a rose with a crowbar. Relationships are like roses: They take time. You can't speed up the process, and you can't force a relationship to grow deeper. Nothing truly beautiful can be manufactured through coercion; it is only through being open and receptive that we discover what nature intends to offer us.

Step 3: Set the container.

A container is the setting, time, and place where we practice. A container is like a bubble that you enter when you want to leave the obligations, distractions, and commitments of the world behind, knowing that they will be there when you return. Inside your container, there is nothing to stop you from fully immersing yourself in whatever you might be doing.

Creating a container requires a certain level of commitment. We practice this commitment by continuously reminding ourselves that we have chosen to be here, and by recognizing negative feelings (for example, fears that we're out of our depth or wasting our time) as judgments that prevent us from experiencing the full potential of our practice. The only thing that completely breaks the container is when we give up and go home.

The first step in building your container is to clear your schedule. Turn off your cell phone, leave it at home, or put it in airplane mode (aka Forest Bathing mode). Eliminate as many distractions as possible; all you need is your body and your attention. You can't rush the process, so give yourself permission to set this time aside. Welcome yourself just as you are, no matter what has happened today, no matter what may happen tomorrow.

Keep yourself open to the many possibilities that have yet to be revealed. Don't begin with the intention of seeking wisdom. Recognize that this moment, too, has its own nature; it is comprised of everything that intersects here and now, and it knows when you will be ready to receive what is has to offer.

Anticipate that some of what will come may feel edgy, but remember that Forest Bathing is not a direct flight to perfect bliss; rather, it is a pathway toward relationship, and the cultivation of real relationships is not always easy. When challenges or fears arise, be aware that not only are they part of the sensation of being alive, they are the pathway to resilience and growth. You are not alone; all beings encounter difficulties along the way.

Finish preparing the container by saying to yourself: "This is about process. I have set this time aside. I have everything I need within me. I have no agenda. I will be open to whatever comes up. I know my own boundaries."

Step 4: Awaken your senses.

Now it is time to stop thinking and start feeling. Don't rush through this step. Devote your full attention to your sensory experience. Let each sensation linger for a while before moving on.

Begin with the breath. What does it feel like to breathe? Notice the sensation of each breath moving in and out of your body. Placing your hands on your rib cage or stomach, notice the relationship between your body and the air you breathe. Notice how the air moves into and through you. Breathe into your cupped hands. What does your breath feel like on the skin?

While sitting or standing, notice how you exist in space. What does it feel like to be in your body? Notice whether your body might be asking you for something, perhaps a stretch or a massage? Perhaps to lay down or to dance? Be generous with yourself by allowing the body to lead you in whatever direction it desires.

And now, simply listen to the world around you. Let your attention move from one sound to the next, welcoming them as they come. Notice the small sounds, big sounds, near and distant sounds. Notice them without judgment. Let your attention linger on each one as it arises and fades away. You might try closing your eyes; I wonder if your hearing will grow stronger. Notice the sound of your breath coming from within your body. How does it blend in with the full soundscape around you?

And now, touch the world. Let your skin explore the textures of whatever you are standing or sitting on, be it leaves, bark, soil, sand, water, or your sofa. Feel the air and sunlight and shadow on your skin. You might try reaching out with cupped hands to simply hold the air; I wonder what it feels like to hold the sky in your hands. Perhaps you have noticed that the sky is also holding you? Consider taking time to experience what it feels like when you touch your skin. You might allow your hands to explore each other, simply noticing.

And now, smell. Flowers, trees, soil, the air. How many smells are there in this place? How many surprising aromas might be discovered with just a tiny bit of curiosity? In some cases, you may need to awaken the smells of the beings around you by simply touching them. Try caressing the leaves or needles of the trees and notice what happens.

And now, taste. Perhaps you sense the lingering taste of something you ate or drank earlier? Perhaps if you breathe in the air as though sipping it through a straw, you might be able to taste it on your palate?

And now, take a good look around. Notice the movement, shapes, color, and light. What does this place really look like? Notice how far into the distance your vision can see, and notice the small details close by. I wonder how many details might be missed when we were not truly looking.

As your imaginal sense awakens, what does your heart begin to notice in this place? What remains hidden beneath the surfaces of your sensory perception? What is speaking directly to you? What is speaking through you, your body, and the world? Gaze out with your heart; can you sense the inner beauty of this moment?

Notice that you are alive and that your body is nature, here in this moment. Notice how your body responds to this attention. Take time to explore the dynamic interplay of sensations arising and fading away. How do they move through you?

And finally, simply notice how you feel in this moment. Whatever feelings arise, offer them hospitality. And if something is offering you a sense of feeling alive, just be with that sensation for a while. Let it reside in your body as you breathe. Welcome it home to the forest of yourself.

Step 5: Slow down.

The forest is in no rush, and neither are we. Take time to wander slowly, allowing your body to lead you where it will. This might feel strange at first because we're not used to moving slowly. Try not to perform slowness, so that the performance becomes your focus, but simply walk slowly with the intention of holding curiosity.

One helpful way to slow down is to take off your shoes and feel the sensations of each step upon your skin. Barefoot, you might also become more aware of how the act of taking a single step sends waves of sensation throughout your entire body. Placing one foot in front of you requires a startling number of micro-adjustments in the body, rippling outward from the core. Moving slowly, you can actually begin to remember what walking feels like in the body. It is quite an amazing thing to experience what most of us take for granted every day!

Linger wherever your senses draw you. You might pause to watch a dragonfly or stop to smell the scent of the pines. You might touch the water running through the creek or listen to the crows cawing. You might begin to notice that your movement is connected to the movement of everything around you. You might touch a tree and notice how your movement extends into the branches and leaves, just as when a bird or squirrel causes motion with the movement of their own bodies. Eventually, you may recognize how this world is like a sort of effortless dance among all beings.

As you practice, continue to ask yourself what *slowness* really means? At first, your slowness may look like the pace of clouds drifting in the sky. As you become more comfortable with slowness, perhaps you will learn to embody the slowness of trees, or maybe even mountains? What would it be like to move as slowly as stone?

Step 6: Relate.

Everything is reaching out to form relationship with your body: every tuft of grass, every tree, every bird and river and cloud in the sky. Take this opportunity to spend time with the individual beings around you. Get to know one being at a time. Resist the temptation to think in abstraction, to assume that one experience will be like all others, and lean into the story that everything, in every moment, is unique.

Get to know these beings with all of your senses, and allow them to know you as well. Be open to receiving invitations from the beings of the earth. Perhaps a stone invites you to hold it in your hands, or a tree beckons for you to lay down beneath its branches? Perhaps the ocean invites you to take time to listen, or the sunlight asks you to dance? Maybe your body quietly asks for a moment to rest, to breathe. Be open to receiving these invitations, and the world will teach you how to love it.

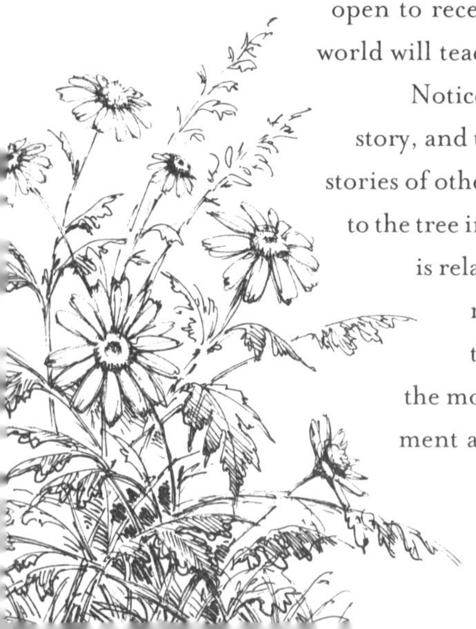

Notice that every being has its own story, and that these stories overlap with the stories of other beings. A single bird is related to the tree in which it builds its nest; this tree is related to the river that waters it; the river is related to the mountains that gather the rain from clouds; the mountains are related to the movement and heat of the sun. Every being exists in a web of relationships that spirals out to every corner of the world, connecting all beings in deep time. As we participate in real relationship with any single being, so too do we cultivate relationship with the whole.

You may also take time to observe the inner beauty of each being. Whether or not you think you are actually capable of such observation, this invitation might lead you to some wonderful discoveries about yourself and your own nature. If you believe that you love nature, then see if you can love each being for the beauty inside it, the beauty that can only be known through intimate and direct experience. To see the inner beauty of the world, just stop thinking about it; release yourself from needing to form opinions or judgments and allow yourself to experience the moment in relationship. Perhaps the depth of your love will surprise you.

If you are practicing in a group, then share what you experience with friends. It can be beautiful to weave human relationships into your exploration of the world, sharing with others whatever invitations reveal themselves to you. Perhaps what nature reveals to you is not meant for you alone, but rather is meant to be a shared gift?

STEP 7: PLAY.

Play allows us to have experiences we never would have anticipated. It is an exploration of what is possible, energized by a limitless curiosity. Let yourself be curious, and, whatever you do, don't overthink how you play; just go for it in whatever way feels right in your body.

First, remember the playfulness of the body. Let your body move freely; let it remember how it wants to play. Jump, dance, climb a tree, lay down and gaze at the clouds, or roll down a hill.

Second, remember the playfulness of nature. Notice how nature plays and how it invites you to play. Skip a stone across the lake, draw a picture in the sand, shower yourself with fallen leaves, or arrange stones and acorn caps in a mosaic upon the earth.

Third, remember the playfulness of your imaginal sense. Lay down and simply be open to the possibility of your mind wandering into a soft reverie. Observe with curiosity where it takes you; you don't need to know what's coming next.

So long as we are authentically engaged, play allows us to feel the aliveness we experienced as children, before we became caught up in the gravity of our thoughts. We don't need to evaluate whether we are playing properly; there are no limits or wrong ways. I wonder what new games the world will reveal to you as you improvise ways of being and loving nature.

Step 8: Be with yourself.

Even when practicing Forest Bathing with friends, it's good to spend some time alone. It doesn't have to be a lot of time; as little as thirty minutes will do. And you won't really be alone, anyway; you're going to be spending time with yourself, your body, and nature.

Alone, you are most capable of abandoning whatever is performative in your relationship to yourself and to nature. Solitude is a place to experience reality without any compulsion to be seen as you wish to be seen; it is the ideal place to explore your deepest authenticity and vulnerability. You can just be as you are. If you want to laugh, then laugh. If you want to cry, then cry. Nature will give you the space to do what you need to do.

Being alone, without the distraction of screens or conversations, can be challenging at first. You will question what exactly you are supposed to be doing. There will be temptation to seek out some kind of mental stimulation to distract yourself from this moment. In solitude, we confront a sense of purposelessness that feels uncomfortable at first but ultimately teaches us important lessons about who we are.

You might be surprised what happens when you sit alone. You may notice that the beings of nature relate to you differently. Animals that scattered upon your arrival may begin to come back and share space with you. Your body may find hidden fascinations that you would have never noticed otherwise. You might rest in such a way that you experience the joy of simply being. You might be astounded at the full range of phenomena in a single sunset, observing each star appear, one by one against the delicately shifting color of the dusk. You might be surprised by how much more you notice when you are alone.

Step 9: Acknowledge.

Before you finish a Forest Bathing session, you might want to express your gratitude, maybe to your friends who have accompanied you on the journey, and maybe to the beings of nature. Find a way to share something about your experience, even if it is silence.

You might consider tending the land in small ways—picking up garbage, for example—to show your gratitude. If you are practicing on the land where you live, perhaps you will feel inspired to support your neighboring beings in ways that suit their interests and lifestyles.

You might also express your gratitude in the form of intentional thoughts, promises to live in better relationship with yourself and with the more than human world. Simply taking a moment to witness the miracle that is you and your interconnectedness to this world can be a powerful gesture. No matter what is happening in the world, you are here, now. You are awake, you are present, you are alive.

There's no right or wrong way. Ask yourself what you can offer.

Step 10: Return.

Say goodbye. Come home safely. If you want to remember your Forest Bathing experiences, consider keeping a journal.

And then, return to where you have spent time and continue to practice. The wonderful thing about Forest Bathing as a relationship-building process is that it never ends. Just as you wouldn't attempt to exhaust the potential of a human relationship in one visit, so it is with nature. Return to the places you have frequented. Sense them in all seasons and at all times of the day. Keep going back, over and over again, and continue to be curious, knowing that you have not yet discovered all of their surprises.

The work of building and tending relationships requires time more than anything else. No matter what you do, there is no shortcut, no way to fast-forward to real

depth of relationship. It's not like learning something with your mind, where you have a *eureka!* moment. It's more like falling in love. You don't even notice that it's happening, but it happens, and you can feel it growing inside of you.

As you cultivate deeper relationships with nature, you will begin to understand that there are no static answers to any of the questions that arise, because relationships are not static. Your relationships won't always grow in a linear fashion; some will take longer than others to develop. Instead of seeking answers, strive to live the questions. Sometimes you won't know what to do, and that's a good thing; it means you're living the question. Keep going.

We notice the deepening of relationship in the body, not in the mind. We feel something indescribable in our hearts, something very personal: a sense that we know and are known by the world. Your relationship with the world has the potential to deepen infinitely. Just like you, the world is always evolving. As the world around us changes, so do we. It's a simple equation. As Ram Dass suggests, "We're all just walking each other home." We're all hand in hand on our journey, returning to what we truly are. All we need to do is remember how to live.

Sit Spot

PROMPT 6

As you sit, invite purposelessness to sit with you. Notice what unfolds around and within you.

CHAPTER 6

FINAL THOUGHTS

Forest Bathing is more than a practice or a technique; it is also a philosophy, a way of perceiving reality. Forest Bathing reminds us that we need not be prisoners of our own abstractions, thoughts, and opinions. We can relate to the world of nature around us through the world of nature within us: our bodies, our senses, and our hearts. We don't have to rely on labels or categories or facts to define what is emergent, dynamic, and alive. We don't even need words for the experiences we encounter as we cultivate real relationships.

Remember, it's simple. Just pay attention—not to your mind, but to your body. If you take only one thing away from this book, please let it be this: Pay attention to your body, and the rest will happen organically in time. The world is happening all around you. Nature never stops. Relationships are found here, in this moment, in community with all beings. At the end of the day, it's all about process, not outcomes. Don't overthink it. Better yet, don't think about it at all.

When we stop thinking, we pause the self-referencing and self-justifying chatter of our egos, and we stop experiencing separateness. In the moments when we are simply here, bathing in the river of time, we wash off whatever labels we've applied to ourselves, and we experience our ecological, original self. Our true identities are always rooted in our interconnectedness with nature. It follows, then, that our most authentic actions are naturally compassionate. When we let go of judgment, we reflexively become predisposed to act with love because we see that any good done for another is good for ourselves as well. We do not arrive at this kind of authentically compassionate action by any force of mental will; it comes when we relax into being what we are.

I don't know what your relationship with nature will look like, but I hope that it serves to bring you closer to real experiences. Real experiences are simply those moments when you are truly present, without any distractions. They are not complicated; they include intimate gestures like feeling the texture of tree bark, hearing birdsong, smelling a wildflower, or gazing at the stars as they turn in the night sky. These experiences are the first steps in any relationship, and it is crucial that we give ourselves time and permission to explore them.

As you explore the kind of aliveness that is shared through real experiences, perhaps your perception will begin to shift. Perhaps real experiences will lead you into real relationships with yourself and your environment. Real relationships reflect the inner beauty of the world. They are grounded in unconditional love. They celebrate all the joy and pain that comes with being nature. It is in these relationships that you will find your true self, your inner nature.

Sit Spot

PROMPT 7

As you sit, invite yourself to sit with you.

Welcome home.

Deep in the canyon
A tree is imagining your return,
A river is remembering your name,
And a pebble is dreaming of you waking up in sunlight.

The whole world is wondering if you can find the gift you left for yourself
Before you were you, before you were anything that you would even recognize.

Deep in the canyon
You are preparing to encounter yourself
And laughing at the thought that you were ever separate from all that is
Your heart opens and sees the circle of time
And it lovingly asks itself how many moons have passed
Since you last witnessed yourself in this universe?

—Ben Page, 2017

MANDALA
An Imprint of MandalaEarth
PO Box 3088
San Rafael, CA 94912
www.MandalaEarth.com

Find us on Facebook: www.facebook.com/MandalaEarth
Follow us on Twitter: @MandalaEarth

Library of Congress Cataloging-in-Publication Data available.

ISBN: 978-1-64722-418-9

Publisher: Raoul Goff
VP of Creative: Chrissy Kwasnik
VP of Manufacturing: Alix Nicholaeff
Designer: Amy DeGrote
Editor: Matt Wise
Managing Editor: Lauren LePera
Senior Production Manager: Greg Steffen
Senior Production Manager, Subsidiary Rights: Lina S. Palma

ROOTS of PEACE REPLANTED PAPER

Mandala Publishing, in association with Roots of Peace, will plant two trees for each tree used in the manufacturing of this book. Roots of Peace is an internationally renowned humanitarian organization dedicated to eradicating land mines worldwide and converting war-torn lands into productive farms and wildlife habitats. Roots of Peace will plant two million fruit and nut trees in Afghanistan and provide farmers there with the skills and support necessary for sustainable land use.

Manufactured in China by Insight Editions

10 9 8 7 6 5 4